KETO

DIET

Ketogenic Diet Coobook: The Ultimate Ketogenic Diet

Guide for Weight Loss With 1 Month Meal Plan

@ Johnny Hale

Published By Adam Gilbin

@ Johnny Hale

Ketogenic Diet Coobook: The Ultimate Ketogenic Diet
Guide for Weight Loss With 1 Month Meal Plan

All Right RESERVED

ISBN 978-1-990053-40-5

.

TABLE OF CONTENTS

Keto Tomato Soup

Ingredients:

- 255ml vegetable stock
- 4tsp olive oil
- 8g erythritol [2]
- 1 pinch of salt
- 1 pinch of pepper
- 820g tomatoes
- 30g vegan margarine
- 1/2 onion (red)
- 1 clove of garlic

Directions:

1. Score the tomatoes crosswise at the base and briefly place in boiling water.
2. Now rinse the tomatoes with cold water and peel off their skin with a knife

3. Now chop the tomatoes and chop the onions, garlic and basil.
4. Briefly sauté the onions, garlic and basil with butter, add the vegetable stock and bring to the boil briefly.
5. Then pour in the tomato pieces and simmer everything for 10 minutes.
6. At the end, pour everything into a mixer and puree.

Cauliflower Rice With Mushrooms

Ingredients:

- 420g cauliflower
- 1 clove of garlic
- 1 onion
- 520g mushrooms)
- 1 tablespoon olive oil
- 255ml vegan white wine (dry)
- 250ml vegetable stock
- 1tsp chilli flakes
- 1 teaspoon thyme (dried)
- 2 tablespoons of truffle oil
- 1 pinch of salt
- 1 pinch of pepper

Directions:

1. First, the cauliflower has to be chopped up using a stand mixer so that it becomes the size of a grain of rice.

2. Then the garlic and onion must be cut into fine cubes. Furthermore, clean the mushrooms and bring them into bite-sized pieces.

3. Now you have to heat the olive oil in a pan and braise the onions and garlic in it. After about 5 minutes add the mushrooms and let them sear again for 5 minutes.

4. Then add the cauliflower rice and deglaze it with white wine and vegetable stock until everything is covered.

5. Now you can season your pan with chilli flakes and thyme and let it simmer for 20 minutes until the liquid is soaked up.

6. Then you can add some truffle oil and season with salt and pepper if you like.

Chili Con Tofu

Ingredients:

- 1 onion
- 1 red chilli pepper
- 205ml vegetable stock
- 2 cloves of garlic
- 2 tablespoons tomato paste
- 2 teaspoons oregano spice
- 1 tablespoon paprika spice sweet
- 1 tablespoon sunflower oil
- If necessary some chilli spice
- 420g tofu (natural)
- 420g pizza tomatoes
- 1 can of kidney beans (approx. 250g drained weight)
- 150g vegetable corn
- 1 red pepper

Directions:

1. First, the peppers must be washed, pitted and diced. In addition, the onion must be peeled and chopped into small pieces.

2. Now prepare the tofu by pressing it into small pieces with a fork.

3. Fry the tofu in a large frying pan with 1 tablespoon of sunflower oil and add onion, paprika and paprika to the tofu.

4. Now fry the whole thing for a few more minutes until the onions are translucent.

5. Then you peel the garlic cloves and press them through the garlic press into the pan.

6. Then add the finely chopped chilli pepper, tomato paste, pizza tomatoes, 2 teaspoons oregano and 205 ml vegetable stock to the tofu.

7. The whole thing must then simmer for 10 minutes with the lid closed.

8. At the end you add the drained kidney beans and the corn and stir your chili con tofu one last time.

Vegan Mayonnaise Se

Ingredients:

- 1tsp Dijon mustard [17]
- 250ml light olive oil
- Salt to taste
- 3 tablespoons aquafaba (chickpea liquid) [24]
- 2 teaspoons of white wine vinegar or lemon juice

Directions:

1. Put the aquafaba (the liquid in a can of cooked chickpeas), vinegar and Dijon mustard in a tall blender or measuring cup.
2. Mix with a hand blender for about 30 seconds on high speed until frothy.
3. Pour in the olive oil in a very slow, thin stream while mixing at full speed.
4. A smooth, creamy emulsion should form.

5. Move the hand blender up and down towards the end to bring in some air to make the mixture fluffier.

6. Try and season with salt.

Keto Coleslaw

Ingredients:

- salt and pepper
- fresh parsley (optional)
- 480g kohlrabi
- 250ml vegan mayonnaise (recipe 158)

Directions:

1. First peel the kohlrabi. Make sure to remove the hard, woody parts.
2. Then finely chop the kohlrabi and put it in a bowl.
3. Add the mayonnaise and optionally fresh herbs.
4. Season to taste with salt and pepper.

Keto Falafel

Ingredients:

- 2 cloves of garlic, chopped
- 2 tablespoons fresh parsley, finely chopped
- 1 teaspoon salt
- 1 teaspoon onion powder
- 1 teaspoon ground cumin
- 1 teaspoon of ground coriander seeds
- 1/2 teaspoon ground black pepper
- 250g mushrooms, sliced
- 130ml light Olivenö l
- 130ml (75g) pumpkin seeds
- 130ml almonds
- 190ml Aquafaba (chickpea liquid) [24]
- 65ml water
- 4 tablespoons (50g) chia seeds [9]

Directions:

1. Preheat the oven to 175 ° C.

2. Heat a large pan and lightly toast the almonds and pumpkin seeds.

3. Fry the mushrooms in a large pan in ⅓ of the olive oil until soft and moist.

4. Put the mushrooms and the remaining oil in the food processor along with the remaining ingredients.

5. Mix this mass for a few minutes. Let rest for 5 minutes.

6. Shape the mixture into 4 cm balls. Place the balls on a baking sheet.

7. Bake in the oven for 20 minutes or wait until they are crispy.

8. Serve warm with the side dish of your choice.

Instant Pot French Onion Soup

Ingredients:

- 1 tablespoon minced garlic
- 1 teaspoon salt
- 1 bay leaf
- 2 cups shredded Gruyère cheese
- 1 tablespoon grass-fed butter
- 2 large white onions, sliced
- 6 cups vegetable broth

Directions:

1. Turn the Instant Pot to sauté mode and melt the butter.
2. Add the onions and allow them to cook until translucent, 4 to 5 minutes.
3. Pour in the broth, garlic, salt, and bay leaf.
4. Cover the pot with its lid (until it clicks closed), and turn the pot to manual pressure for 25 minutes.

5. Once the timer goes off, turn the Instant Pot off and allow it to natural-release for 10 to 15 minutes.

6. Then release any additional pressure. Divide the soup between six bowls.

7. Sprinkle the cheese on each bowl of soup and serve hot.

Creamed Cauliflower Soup

Ingredients:

- 2 cups vegetable broth
- 1 bay leaf
- 1 cup grated sharp Cheddar cheese
- 1 cup heavy (whipping) cream
- 1 teaspoon salt
- 1 teaspoon freshly ground black pepper
- 2 tablespoons grass-fed butter
- 1 white onion, chopped
- 1 tablespoon minced fresh garlic
- 1 medium cauliflower, chopped into small florets

Directions:

1. In a stockpot over medium-high heat, melt the butter.
2. Add the onion and garlic and sauté for about 3 minutes.

3. Add the cauliflower florets and cook, stirring, for another 2 to 3 minutes.
4. Pour in the vegetable broth and add the bay leaf.
5. Bring to a simmer and cook for about 20 minutes, or until the cauliflower is tender.
6. Remove from the heat and stir in the Cheddar cheese, cream, salt, and pepper. Stir until the cheese is totally melted.
7. Divide into 4 portions and serve.

Beef Stew

Ingredients:

- 1 cup diced tomatoes
- 1/2 cup apple cider vinegar
- 2 cups cubed pumpkin, cut into 1-inch chunks
- 1 sweet onion, chopped
- 2 teaspoons minced garlic
- 1 teaspoon dried thyme
- 1 tablespoon chopped fresh parsley, for garnish
- 3 tablespoons extra-virgin olive oil, divided
- 1 (2-pound / 907-g) beef chuck roast, cut into 1-inch chunks
- 1 teaspoon salt
- 1/2 teaspoon freshly ground black pepper
- 2 cups beef broth

Directions:

1. Lightly grease the insert of the slow cooker with 1 tablespoon of the olive oil.
2. Lightly season the beef chucks with salt and pepper.
3. In a large skillet over medium-high heat, heat the remaining 2 tablespoons of the olive oil.
4. Add the beef and brown on all sides, about 7 minutes.
5. Transfer the beef to the insert and stir in the broth, tomatoes, apple cider vinegar, pumpkin, onion, garlic, and thyme.
6. Cover and cook on low heat for about 8 hours, until the beef is very tender.
7. Serve topped with the parsley.

Chicken Stew

Ingredients:

- 2 celery stalks, diced
- 1 carrot, diced
- 1 teaspoon dried thyme
- 1 cup shredded kale
- 1 cup coconut cream
- Salt, for seasoning
- Freshly ground black pepper, for seasoning
- 3 tablespoons extra-virgin olive oil, divided
- 1 pound (460 g) boneless chicken thighs, diced into 2-inch pieces
- 1 sweet onion, chopped
- 2 teaspoons minced garlic
- 2 cups chicken broth

Directions:

1. Lightly grease the insert of the slow cooker with 1 tablespoon of the olive oil.

2. In a large skillet over medium-high heat, heat the remaining 2 tablespoons of the olive oil.

3. Add the chicken and sauté until it is just cooked through, about 7 minutes.

4. Add the onion and garlic and sauté for an additional 3 minutes.

5. Transfer the chicken mixture to the insert, and stir in the broth, celery, carrot, and thyme.

6. Cover and cook on low for 6 hours.

7. Stir in the kale and coconut cream.

8. Season with salt and pepper, and serve warm.

Curried Vegetable Stew

Ingredients:

- 1 sweet onion, chopped
- 2 teaspoons grated fresh ginger
- 2 teaspoons minced garlic
- 1 tablespoon curry powder
- 2 cups shredded spinach
- 1 avocado, diced, for garnish
- 1 tablespoon extra-virgin olive oil
- 4 cups coconut milk
- 1 cup diced pumpkin
- 1 cup cauliflower florets
- 1 red bell pepper, diced
- 1 zucchini, diced

Directions:

1. Lightly grease the insert of the slow cooker with the olive oil.

2. Add the coconut milk, pumpkin, cauliflower, bell pepper, zucchini, onion, ginger, garlic, and curry powder.
3. Cover and cook on low for 7 to 8 hours.
4. Stir in the spinach.
5. Garnish each bowl with a spoonful of avocado and serve.

Turkey-Vegetable Stew

Ingredients:

- 2 celery stalks, chopped
- 2 cups diced pumpkin
- 1 carrot, diced
- 2 teaspoons chopped thyme
- Salt, for seasoning
- 3 tablespoons extra-virgin olive oil, divided
- 1 pound (454 g) boneless turkey breast, cut into 1-inch pieces
- 1 leek, thoroughly cleaned and sliced
- 2 teaspoons minced garlic
- 2 cups chicken broth
- 1 cup coconut milk
- Freshly ground black pepper, for seasoning
- 1 scallion, white and green parts, chopped, for garnish

Directions:

1. Lightly grease the insert of the slow cooker with 1 tablespoon of the olive oil.
2. In a large skillet over medium-high heat, heat the remaining 2 tablespoons of the olive oil.
3. Add the turkey and sauté until browned, about 5 minutes.
4. Add the leek and garlic and sauté for an additional 3 minutes.
5. Transfer the turkey mixture to the insert and stir in the broth, coconut milk, celery, pumpkin, carrot, and thyme.
6. Cover and cook on low for 7 to 8 hours.
7. Season with salt and pepper.
8. Serve topped with the scallion.

Lamb Stew

Ingredients:

- 1 large red onion, diced
- 1 tablespoon olive oil
- 3 lamb shanks
- 1 lemon, halved and seeded
- 1 cup black olives, pitted
- 4 cups lamb or chicken broth
- 4 cups water
- 1 (32-ounce / 907-g) can crushed tomatoes
- 1 bouquet garni package (thyme, oregano, parsley, bay leaf), tied with twine

Directions:

1. In a large pot over medium-high heat, combine the broth, water, tomatoes, bouquet garni, and onion. Cover.
2. Heat the olive oil in a large skillet over medium-high heat until shimmering.

3. Add the lamb shanks and sear for 3 minutes on each side.
4. Add the seared lamb to the pot and bring almost to a boil.
5. Reduce the heat to medium-low and simmer gently for 2 hours.
6. Squeeze the lemon juice directly into the pot.
7. Add the lemon halves to the pot along with the olives.
8. Cook uncovered for 15 minutes.
9. Remove from the heat and let the stew rest for 15 minutes.
10. Remove and discard the bouquet garni and lemon halves.
11. Pull the meat from the bones. Discard the bones or save for making stock. Serve.

Chipotle Chicken Chili

Ingredients:

- 1 cup chicken broth
- 1 cup diced pumpkin
- 1 green bell pepper, diced
- 3 tablespoons chili powder
- 1 teaspoon chipotle chili powder
- 1 cup sour cream, for garnish
- 1 cup shredded Cheddar cheese, for garnish
- 3 tablespoons extra-virgin olive oil, divided
- 1 pound (454 g) ground chicken
- 1 sweet onion, chopped
- 2 teaspoons minced garlic
- 1 (28-ounce / 794-g) can diced tomatoes

Directions:

1. Lightly grease the insert of the slow cooker with 1 tablespoon of the olive oil.

2. In a large skillet over medium-high heat, heat the remaining 2 tablespoons of the olive oil.

3. Add the chicken and sauté until it is cooked through, about 6 minutes.

4. Add the onion and garlic and sauté for an additional 3 minutes.

5. Transfer the chicken mixture to the insert and stir in the tomatoes, broth, pumpkin, bell pepper, chili powder, and chipotle chili powder.

6. Cover and cook on low for 7 to 8 hours.

7. Serve topped with the sour cream and cheese.

Texas Chili

Ingredients:

- 1 (28-ounce / 794-g) can diced tomatoes
- 1 cup beef broth
- 3 tablespoons chili powder
- 1 teaspoon ground cumin
- 1/2 teaspoon ground coriander
- 1 cup sour cream, for garnish
- 1 avocado, diced, for garnish
- 1 tablespoon cilantro, chopped, for garnish
- 1/2 cup extra-virgin olive oil
- 2 pounds (680 g) beef sirloin, cut into 1-inch chunks
- 1 sweet onion, chopped
- 2 green bell peppers, chopped
- 1 jalapeño pepper, seeded, finely chopped
- 2 teaspoons minced garlic

Directions:

1. Lightly grease the insert of the slow cooker with 1 tablespoon of the olive oil.
2. In a large skillet over medium-high heat, heat the remaining 2 tablespoons of the olive oil.
3. Add the beef and sauté until it is cooked through, about 8 minutes.
4. Add the onion, bell peppers, jalapeño pepper, and garlic, and sauté for an additional 4 minutes.
5. Transfer the beef mixture to the insert and stir in the tomatoes, broth, chili powder, cumin, and coriander.
6. Cover and cook on low for 7 to 8 hours.
7. Serve topped with the sour cream, avocado, and cilantro.

Buffalo Chili

Ingredients:

- 1 (15-ounce / 425-g) can roasted tomatoes
- 1 (15-ounce / 425-g) can tomato sauce (no sugar added)
- 1 cup beef broth
- 1/2 cup chili powder
- 1 tablespoon ground cumin
- 1 teaspoon sea salt
- 1 tablespoon coconut oil
- 2 pounds (907 g) ground bison meat
- 1 large poblano pepper, diced
- 1 large onion, diced
- 3 garlic cloves, minced

Toppings (Optional):

- Grass-fed shredded cheese
- Sour cream
- Avocado

Directions:

1. Heat the coconut oil in a large stockpot over medium heat.

2. Add the bison meat and cook for 8 to 10 minutes, or until browned.

3. Add the pepper, onion, and garlic to the pot. Stir well and cook for 10 minutes.

4. Stir in the tomatoes, tomato sauce, and broth.

5. Add the chili powder, cumin, and salt.

6. Bring to a boil, stir well, reduce the heat to low, and cover.

7. Let it simmer for about 1 hour, stirring occasionally.

8. Serve in bowls with the toppings (if using).

Chicken Chorizo Chili

Ingredients:

- 6 ounces (170 g) tomato paste
- 2 cups bone broth or chicken stock
- 1 jalapeño, diced
- 1/2 cup chili powder
- 3 tablespoons cumin
- 1 teaspoon cayenne
- 1 tablespoon sea salt
- 1 tablespoon apple cider vinegar
- 1 tablespoon avocado oil
- 1 bell pepper, diced
- 1 yellow onion, diced
- 1 pound (454 g) ground chicken
- 1 pound (454 g) chicken chorizo sausage, chopped
- 1 (15-ounce / 425-g) can organic fire-roasted tomatoes

Directions:

1. Heat the avocado oil in a medium skillet over medium heat.

2. Sauté the bell pepper and yellow onion for 4 to 5 minutes, or until the vegetables are tender.

3. Add the ground chicken and chicken sausage, and cook for 6 to 8 minutes, or until browned.

4. Add the fire-roasted tomatoes, tomato paste, and broth. Stir well.

5. Add the jalapeño, chili powder, cumin, cayenne, salt, and vinegar.

6. Stir well and bring to a boil. Reduce the heat to low and simmer for 1 hour.

7. Serve the chili in bowls.

Hot Swiss Chard And Artichoke Dip

Ingredients:

- 1 cup shredded Cheddar cheese
- 1 teaspoon minced garlic
- Dash hot sauce (optional)
- 2 cups chopped Swiss chard
- 1 cup roughly chopped artichoke hearts (packed in brine, not oil)
- 4 ounces (113 g) cream cheese, at room temperature
- 1 cup coconut milk
- 1 cup grated Asiago cheese

Directions:

1. Preheat the oven. Set the oven temperature to 450ºF (235ºC).
2. Mix the ingredients. In a large bowl, stir together the cream cheese, coconut milk, Asiago, Cheddar, garlic, and hot sauce (if using), until everything is well mixed.

3. Stir in the chard and the artichoke hearts and mix until they're well incorporated.

Stuffed Mushrooms With Crab

Ingredients:

- 1 scallion, chopped
- 1 tablespoon chopped fresh parsley
- 1 teaspoon minced garlic
- 12 large button mushrooms, cleaned and stemmed
- Olive oil cooking spray
- 1 cup cooked chopped crab
- 1 cup cream cheese, softened
- 1 cup grated Parmesan cheese
- 1/2 cup ground almonds

Directions:

1. Preheat the oven. Set the oven temperature to 375ºF (190ºC). Line a baking sheet with parchment paper.

2. Mix the filling. In a large bowl, stir together the crab, cream cheese, Parmesan, almonds,

scallion, parsley, and garlic until everything is well mixed.

3. Precook the mushrooms. Place the mushrooms stem-side up on the baking sheet and lightly spray them with olive oil.

4. Bake them for 2 minutes then drain them stem-side down on paper towels.

5. Stuff the mushrooms. Turn the mushrooms over and place them back on the baking sheet.

6. Spoon about 1½ tablespoons of the filling into each mushroom.

7. Bake the mushrooms. Bake for 15 minutes until the mushrooms are lightly golden and bubbly.

8. Serve. Arrange the mushrooms on a serving platter.

Warm Thyme Olives

Ingredients:

- 1 teaspoon dried thyme
- 1/2teaspoon fennel seeds
- Pinch red pepper flakes
- 1/2 cup olive oil
- 4 ounces (120 g) green olives
- 4 ounces (120 g) Kalamata olives

Directions:

1. Sauté the olives. In a large skillet over medium heat, warm the olive oil.
2. Sauté the olives, thyme, fennel seeds, and red pepper flakes until the olives start to brown, 3 to 4 minutes.
3. Serve. Put the olives into a bowl and serve them warm.

Lemon Grilled Kale

Ingredients:

- 7 cups large kale leaves, thoroughly washed and patted dry
- Sea salt, for seasoning
- Freshly ground black pepper, for seasoning
- 1 cup olive oil
- 2 teaspoons freshly squeezed lemon juice
- 1 teaspoon garlic powder

Directions:

1. Preheat the grill. Set the grill to medium-high heat.
2. Mix the dressing. In a large bowl, whisk together the olive oil, lemon juice, and garlic powder until it thickens.
3. Prepare the kale. Add the kale leaves to the bowl and use your fingers to massage the dressing thoroughly all over the leaves.
4. Season the leaves lightly with salt and pepper.

5. Grill and serve. Place the kale leaves in a single layer on the preheated grill.

6. Grill for 1 to 2 minutes, turn the leaves over, and grill the other side for 1 minute, until they're crispy.

7. Put the leaves on a platter and serve.

Coconut Creamed Spinach

Ingredients:

- 1/2 cup coconut cream
- 1/4teaspoon ground nutmeg
- Pinch sea salt
- Pinch freshly ground black pepper
- 1 tablespoon grass-fed butter
- 1/52 onion, thinly sliced
- 4 cups coarsely chopped spinach, thoroughly washed
- 1 cup vegetable broth

Directions:

1. Cook the onion. In a large skillet over medium heat, melt the butter.
2. Add the onion and sauté until it's softened, about 2 minutes.
3. Cook the spinach. Stir in the spinach, vegetable broth, coconut cream, nutmeg, salt, and pepper and cook, giving it a stir from time

to time, until the spinach is tender and the sauce thickens, about 15 minutes.

4. Serve. Put the creamed spinach in a bowl and serve.

Vegetable Sauté

Ingredients:

- 1 red bell pepper, cut into thick slices
- 1 yellow bell pepper, cut into thick slices
- Sea salt, for seasoning
- Freshly ground black pepper, for seasoning
- 2 tablespoons grass-fed butter
- 1 tablespoon olive oil
- 2 teaspoons minced garlic
- 2 zucchini, cut into ¼-inch rounds

Directions:

1. Cook the vegetables. In a large skillet over medium-high heat, warm the butter and olive oil.
2. Add the garlic and sauté it for 2 minutes.
3. Add the zucchini and the red and yellow bell peppers to the skillet and sauté, stirring from time to time, for 7 minutes.

4. Serve. Season the vegetables with salt and pepper, spoon them into a bowl, and serve.

Baked Cauliflower Buffalo Bites

Ingredients:

- 2 tablespoons grass-fed butter, melted
- 1 tablespoon coconut flour
- 1 head cauliflower, cut into small florets
- 2 cup hot sauce, divided
- 1 cup chicken stock

Directions:

1. Preheat the oven. Set the oven temperature to 450ºF (235ºC).
2. Line a baking sheet with parchment paper.
3. Prepare the sauce. In a large bowl, whisk together the hot sauce, chicken stock, melted butter, and coconut flour until everything is well blended.
4. Prepare the cauliflower.
5. Add the cauliflower florets to the sauce and stir to get them completely coated with sauce.

6. Bake and serve. Spread the cauliflower on the baking sheet and bake until it's tender, about 20 minutes.

7. Put the cauliflower in a bowl and serve.

Simple Grilled Asparagus

Ingredients:

- 2 tablespoons olive oil
- Sea salt, for seasoning
- Freshly ground black pepper, for seasoning
- 1 pound (480 g) fresh asparagus spears, woody ends snapped off

Directions:

1. Preheat the grill. Set the grill to high heat.
2. Prepare the asparagus. In a medium bowl, toss the asparagus spears with the olive oil and season them with salt and pepper.
3. Grill and serve. Grill the asparagus until tender, 2 to 4 minutes.
4. Arrange them on a platter and serve.

Garlic Wild Mushrooms With Bacon

Ingredients:

- 2 teaspoons minced garlic
- 2 tablespoons chicken stock
- 1 tablespoon chopped fresh thyme
- 6 strips uncured bacon, chopped
- 4 cups sliced wild mushrooms

Directions:

1. Cook the bacon. In a large skillet over medium-high heat, cook the bacon until it's crispy and cooked through, about 7 minutes.
2. Cook the mushrooms.
3. Add the mushrooms and garlic and sauté until the mushrooms are tender, about 7 minutes.
4. Deglaze the pan. Add the chicken stock and stir to scrape up any browned bits in the bottom of the pan.

5. Garnish and serve. Put the mushrooms in a bowl, sprinkle them with the thyme, and serve.

Keto Fried Chicken

Ingredients:

- 2 Large Eggs
- 1/4 cup of Heavy Cream
- 1/4 cup of Water
- 3/4 inch of Deep Hot Oil
- 1/8 teaspoon of Coarse Black Pepper
- 10 pieces of Chicken
- 2 cup of Plain Whey Protein
- 1 cup of Crushed Pork Rinds
- 1/2 teaspoon of Onion Powder
- 1 tablespoon of Oat Fiber
- 1/2 cup of Parmesan Cheese

Directions:

1. Measure out and then mix together all your dry ingredients in a paper bag. Shake it well.
2. Whisk eggs, water, and cream together in your large-sized bowl.

3. Toss in your pieces of cut up chicken into your egg mix and coat each piece completely.

4. Take pieces out of your bowl and drop in your bag of seasoned flour.

5. When 3 pieces are in your bag, hold the top closed and shake your bag to coat chicken.

6. Heat 3/4-inch deep oil on a high heat.

7. Place your pieces close together. Lower the heat to a medium-high.

8. Brown your chicken on one side. Turn over carefully and brown the opposite side. Should take approximately 30 minutes.

9. Remove and place on your paper towel.

10. Serve!

Keto Chicken Divan

Ingredients:

- 3 cups of Cauliflower
- 1 teaspoon of Lemon Juice
- 1/2 cup of Mayonnaise
- 1 cup of Heavy Cream
- 2 cups of Shredded Cheddar Cheese
- 10 cranks of Fresh Pepper
- 1/2 teaspoon of Garlic Salt
- Dash of Parsley
- 2 Boneless Chicken Breasts
- 3 tablespoons of Ghee
- 1 Small Yellow Onion
- 3 cups of Steamed Chopped Broccoli
- 1/2 tablespoon of Minced Garlic
- 1 cup of Chicken Stock or Broth

Directions:

1. Preheat your oven to 350 degrees.

2. Fill your pot halfway with water. Add in your chicken breasts.

3. Cook on high heat and bring to a boil until your chicken is cooked.

4. Cook your onions and garlic in a medium frying pan over a low heat with your ghee.

5. While that cooks, blend your cauliflower using your food processor. Do this for a few seconds until it looks like rice.

6. After cooking your onions for 2 minutes, add in your spices one by one mixing each one in.

7. Once your onions are nice and soft, add in your cauliflower.

8. Once your cauliflower gets soft, add in your chicken broth. Cover and cook for approximately 10 minutes.

9. Take out your chicken once it's done.

10. Add your lemon juice and cream. Allow it to simmer uncovered over a low heat for approximately 10 minutes. Mix a few times so your bottom doesn't burn.

11. Add in your mayo and mix. Turn off your burner.

12. Pull your chicken apart.

13. Add in half of your pulled chicken into cauliflower cream mix.

14. Use other 1/2 to line your 8x8-inch casserole dish.

15. On top of your bottom chicken layer, place your steamed chopped broccoli.

16. Top with your cauliflower cream mix.

17. Top that with your cheddar cheese.

18. Place in oven for approximately 30 minutes. Cover it with tinfoil.

19. Remove your tinfoil and cook for approximately 10 minutes.

20. Serve!

Bolognese Zoodle Bake

Ingredients:

Bolognese Sauce:

- 1/2 teaspoon of Thyme

- 1/4 cup of Chicken Bouillon Paste

- 1/2 teaspoon of Ground Marjoram

- 1/2 teaspoon of Ground Nutmeg

- 2 tablespoons of Heavy Whipping Cream

- Salt

- Pepper

- 1 1/2 pounds of Ground Beef

- 1/2 Medium White Onion

- 1 tablespoon of Olive Oil

- 2 cups of Rao's Marinara Sauce

- 3 cloves of Minced Garlic

Zucchini Noodles:

- 1 cup of Shredded Mozzarella Cheese

- Salt

- Pepper
- Fresh Basil (Optional)
- 3 Medium Zucchini
- 2 tablespoons of Olive Oil

Directions:

1. Preheat your skillet over a medium heat and set your slow cooker on "low." Finely dice half of your medium-sized white onion while you wait for your skillet to heat up.

2. Add your olive oil to your frying pan.

3. Once your oil becomes hot, add your diced onion. Cook until your onions start to become translucent and pick up a bit of color.

4. Stir in your minced garlic cloves.

5. Crumble your ground beef into the pan. Don't worry too much about breaking up the chunks as they cook. Everything is going to fall apart in the slow cooker anyway.

6. Add in 1/2 a teaspoon of thyme, 1/2 a teaspoon of nutmeg, 1/2 a teaspoon of marjoram, and black pepper.

7. Mix everything together and allow your beef to cook until it has mostly browned.

8. Mix in 2 cups of Rao's basil tomato marinara sauce.

9. Stir in 2 tablespoons of your heavy whipping cream.

10. Finish the sauce by mixing in 1/4 of a cup of your chicken bouillon.

11. Turn the heat off and allow the sauce to rest for approximately 10 minutes before transferring it into the preheated slow cooker.

12. Be careful not to pour hot sauce into cold stoneware.

13. Cover your slow cooker and allow your sauce to simmer for about 8 hours.

14. Stir occasionally to prevent burning.

15. After the sauce has finished cooking you can season with additional salt if needed.

16. Preheat your oven to 350 degrees.

17. Set up a vegetable spiralizer. Use it to process the zucchini into noodles, and place the noodles in a casserole dish. Break apart the longer strands so that none of them are too long.

18. Add 2 tablespoons of olive oil to your noodles. Season to taste and then mix together.

19. Spread your Bolognese sauce over the top of your zucchini.

20. Top your casserole with 1 cup of shredded mozzarella cheese.

21. If baking right after cooking the Bolognese sauce, then you will only need to heat the casserole in the oven for approximately 15 to 20 minutes.

22. If you've made the sauce ahead of time and it's been chilled in the refrigerator then you will need to bake for 30 to 35 minutes.

23. Garnish with fresh basil if desired.

24. Serve!

Skillet Browned Chicken W/ Creamy Greens

Ingredients:

- 1 cup of Cream
- 1 teaspoon of Italian Herbs
- 2 tablespoons of Coconut Flour
- 2 cups of Dark Leafy Greens
- Pepper
- Salt
- 1 pound of Boneless Chicken Thighs
- 1 cup of Chicken Stock

- 2 tablespoons of Coconut Oil
- 2 tablespoons of Melted Butter

Directions:

1. Preheat your large-sized skillet on a medium-high setting.
2. Add 2 tablespoons of coconut oil to your pan.
3. Season both sides of your chicken thighs with salt and pepper while your oil heats up.
4. Brown your chicken thighs in the skillet.
5. Fry both sides until your chicken is cooked through and crispy.
6. While your thighs are cooking you should start the sauce.
7. To create your sauce, melt 2 tablespoons of butter in your saucepan.
8. Once your butter stops sizzling, whisk in 2 tablespoons of coconut flour to form a thick paste.
9. Whisk in 1 cup of cream and bring your mixture to a boil.

10. The mixture should thicken after a few minutes. Stir in the teaspoon of Italian herbs.

11. Remove your cooked chicken thighs from the skillet and set to the side.

12. Pour the cup of chicken stock into your chicken skillet and deglaze the pan.

13. Whisk in your cream sauce. Stir the greens into your pan so that they become coated with your sauce.

14. Lay your chicken thighs back on top of the greens, then remove from the heat and serve.

15. Divide your chicken and greens up into 4 servings.

16. Serve!

Chicken Roulades W/ Sage & Gruyere

Ingredients:

- 1 tablespoon of Butter
- 3 ounces of Gruyere Cheese (Finely Grated)
- 1 tablespoon of White Wine Vinegar
- 2 tablespoons + 1 teaspoon of Chopped Fresh Sage
- 2 Chicken Breasts
- 1 Diced Medium Onion
- Salt
- Pepper

Directions:

1. Preheat your oven to 375 degrees. Line an 11x13-inch baking pan with your parchment paper.
2. Butterfly each chicken breast.

3. Place your knife along the side of the breast and use a sawing motion to carefully slice through the side, like opening a bagel.

4. Be careful not to slice completely through the other side.

5. Open the breast and lay flat.

6. Sandwich each of your chicken breasts between two pieces of plastic wrap.

7. Using a meat tenderizing mallet, pound each breast until it is flat and about 1/4-inch thick.

8. Sprinkle each side lightly with your salt and pepper.

9. Heat a medium-sized skillet over a medium heat. Add your butter.

10. When your butter stops foaming, add your onions to your skillet.

11. Cook your onions over a medium-low heat until they caramelize, stirring frequently.

12. Add your white wine vinegar and stir, scraping up the browned bits.

13. When the vinegar becomes syrupy, remove your pan from the heat.

14. Add 2 tablespoons of sage and stir to combine. Season to taste with your salt and pepper.

15. Lay out three pieces of twine and place your flattened chicken breast on top.

16. Keeping the filling away from the edges, spread 1/2 of your onion sage mixture on each chicken breast.

17. Sprinkle 2 ounces of grated cheese over each breast, reserving 1 ounce for later.

18. Roll each breast and secure tightly with twine or toothpicks.

19. Place in your baking pan and make sure they do not touch.

20. Sprinkle your reserved cheese and sage over the roulades.

21. Bake in your preheated oven for pproximately 35 minutes or until your chicken is cooked

through. If the top is not sufficiently brown, place your chicken under the broiler for a few minutes at the end of cooking.

22. Watch carefully as the cheese will brown quickly.

23. Remove from your oven and allow to cool for about 5 minutes before slicing.

24. Remove your twine or toothpicks from the roulades.

25. Carefully slice in a crosswise fashion.

26. Serve!

Bbq Bacon Cheeseburger Waffles

Ingredients:

Waffles:

- 1 cup of Cauliflower Crumbles

- 1/4 teaspoon of Onion Powder

- 1/4 teaspoon of Garlic Powder

- Salt

- Pepper

- 1 1/2 ounces of Cheddar Cheese

- 3 tablespoons of Parmesan Cheese

- 2 Large Eggs

- 4 tablespoons of Almond Flour

Topping:

- 4 slices of Chopped Bacon

- 4 tablespoons of Sugar-Free BBQ Sauce

- 1 1/2 ounces of Cheddar Cheese

- 4 ounces of Ground Beef (70/30)

- Salt

- Pepper

Directions:

1. Shred up 3 ounces worth of cheese.

2. Half will go into your waffle and half will go on top, so make sure you keep it to the side.

3. Mix in half of your cheddar cheese, Parmesan cheese, eggs, almond flour, and spices. Set to the side.

4. Slice your bacon thin and cook over a medium-high heat.

5. Once your bacon is partially cooked, add in your beef.

6. Add any excess grease from your pan into your waffle mixture that you have set to the side.

7. Immersion blend your waffle mixture into a thick paste.

8. Add half of your mixture to your waffle iron and cook until it's crisp.

9. Keep in mind that cauliflower waffles tend to take a little bit longer to cook (there's much more moisture).

10. A good rule of thumb to use is that the waffle is finished once there is little to no steam coming from the waffle iron.

11. Repeat for the second waffle.

12. While your waffles are cooking, add in your sugar-free BBQ sauce to the bacon and ground beef mixture in your pan.

13. Assemble your waffles together by adding half of the ground beef mixture and half of the remaining cheddar cheese to the top of your waffle.

14. Broil for 1 to 2 minutes or until your cheese is nicely melted over the top.

15. Slice up your green onion while your pizzas are broiling to sprinkle over the top.

16. Serve!

Chicken Thighs W/ Spinach

Ingredients:

- 2 cups of Water
- Garlic
- Salt
- Pepper
- 16 Boneless Chicken Thighs (Skinless)
- 2 tablespoons of Shredded Cheddar Cheese
- 24 ounces of Spinach

Directions:

1. Place your chicken thighs into your roaster pan covered with your lid.
2. Bake at 350 degrees for approximately 2 hours.
3. Remove and allow it to cool.
4. Place 2 thighs each in 8 different containers.
5. Break up your thighs and place your vegetables and cheese on each.

6. Distribute your leftover juices over the chicken in each container.

7. Serve!

Loaded Baked Chicken

Ingredients:

- 4 ounces of Cheddar Cheese
- 4 ounces of Ranch Dressing
- 3 Green Onions
- 4 Chicken Breasts
- 4 Bacon Strips
- 1 ounce of Soy Sauce

Directions:

1. Heat your cast iron pan and cook your oil on a high heat.
2. Pan fry your chicken breasts. Flip them half way through.
1. Total cook time should be approximately 10 to 15 minutes.
2. Internal temperature should be 165 degrees.
3. While your chicken cooks, cook your bacon and crumble into bits when done.

4. Chop up your green onions.

5. Place your chicken in your baking dish.

6. Top it with your soy sauce, then add your ranch, bacon, green onions, and your cheese.

7. Broil on high for approximately 3 to 4 minutes until your cheese melts.

8. Serve!

Beer Can Chicken

Ingredients:

- 1 can of Beer
- Rotisserie Seasoning
- 1 Whole Chicken
- 1 tablespoon of Bacon Fat

Directions:

1. Preheat your grill to a medium-high heat, Set it up for indirect grilling. No heat under the chicken.
2. Remove and get rid of your gizzards from your thawed chicken.
3. Cut away the loose skin and chicken parts from the opening of breast cavity.
4. Dry it on both the outside and inside.
5. Apply oil or bacon fat to the outside of your chicken.

6. Rub in your Rotisserie seasoning on both inside and outside.

7. Remove half of the beer from the can and set your chicken on the can.

8. Grill for approximately 60 minutes or until your meat reads between 165 and 180 degrees.

9. Allow it to rest for 5 to 10 minutes.

10. Serve!

Garlic Lebanese Chicken Thighs

Ingredients:

- 1 Juiced Fresh Lemon
- Handful of Baby Carrots
- Garlic Olive Oil
- Oregano
- Pepper
- Salt
- 4 Chicken Thighs
- 1 Vidalia Onion (Quartered)
- 2 Roma Tomatoes
- 2 tablespoons of Ghee
- 15 whole cloves of Garlic

Directions:

1. Heat your oven to 500 degrees.
2. Glaze the bottom of your cast iron pan with 2 teaspoons of garlic olive oil.

3. Add your 4 chicken thighs together. Make sure some space separate them.

4. Wedge your carrots, onions, tomatoes, and garlic cloves between your chicken thighs.]

5. Add 2 garlic cloves on top of the thighs.

6. Juice your lemon over your chicken thighs.

7. Drizzle more garlic oil over the top of your chicken thighs.

8. Drizzle ghee over your chicken thighs.

9. Sprinkle your oregano over your dish. Add your pepper and salt.

10. Place in oven for approximately 30 minutes.

11. Reduce your heat to 350 degrees and then cook approximately 20 minutes until cooked to an internal temperature of 165 degrees.

12. Place your oven on broil and cook an additional 5 minutes until outside the skin is crispy.

13. Remove from your oven.

14. Serve!

Tequila Chicken

Ingredients:

Marinade:

- 1/4 cup of Soy Sauce
- 2 tablespoons of Lime Juice
- 1 shot of Tequila (50 ml)
- 1/2 teaspoon of Salt
- 6 Chicken Breasts
- 1/2 teaspoon of Garlic Powder
- 1 cup of Water
- 1/2 teaspoon of Liquid Smoke

Sauce:

- 1/4 teaspoon of Dried Parsley
- 6 ounces of Shredded Cheddar Cheese
- 1/4 teaspoon of Paprika
- 1/4 teaspoon of Chili Powder
- 1/4 teaspoon of Ground Cumin
- 1/4 teaspoon of Salt

- 1/4 teaspoon of Black Pepper

- 1/4 cup of Sour Cream

- 1/4 cup of Tomato Sauce

- 1/4 cup of Mayonnaise

- 1/4 teaspoon of Frank's Hot Sauce

- 1 tablespoon of Heavy Cream

- 1/4 teaspoon of Dried Dill

- 1/4 teaspoon of Cayenne Pepper

Directions:

1. Mix together your marinade ingredients.

2. Add your chicken to the marinade. Allow it to sit and refrigerate for approximately 2 to 3 hours.

3. Place your chicken on your broiler pan and then broil for approximately 20 minutes on high. Flip it after 10 minutes.

4. Check chicken for temperature. You want it to get to 165 degrees internally.

5. Mix all your ingredients for your sauce except the cheese.

6. Place your meat in your casserole dish. Cover it with sauce and your cheese.

7. Broil for 3 more minutes on high. Cheese should be a little bubbly.

8. Serve!

Pounded Chicken Pizza

Ingredients:

- 2 ounces of Shredded Cheddar Cheese
- 1/2 cup of Marinara Sauce
- 1 ounce of Shredded Monterey Cheese
- Italian Seasoning
- Pepper
- Salt
- 4 Chicken Thighs
- 16 slices of Pepperoni
- 2 ounces of Shredded Jarlsberg Cheese
- 4 slices of Bacon

Directions:

1. Preheat your oven to 350 degrees.
2. Start cooking your 4 slices of bacon.
3. Place your chicken thighs on cutting board. Cover it with saran wrap. Pound it with your heavy pan.

4. Pepper and salt both sides of your chicken.

5. Heat up grease in your pan over a high heat. Sear your chicken on each side for 1 minute.

6. Transfer your skillet to your oven and cook for approximately 10 minutes.

7. Remove your skillet from the oven. Add your seasoning and sauce.

8. Cover it with cheese and place back in your oven for approximately 3 minutes on broil.

9. Remove from oven. Add your remaining toppings.

10. This includes pepperoni and bacon. Broil for 2 more minutes.

11. Serve!

Beer Can Burgers

Ingredients:

- 6 ounces of Cooked Sliced Fresh Mushrooms

- 6 ounces of Cooked Brussels Sprouts

- 6 ounces of Cooked Green Peppers

- 6 ounces of Cooked Onions

- 50 ounces of Ground Beef

- 2 ounces of Pepper Jack Cheese (Cubed)

- 10 slices of Bacon

- 2 ounces of Shredded Extra Sharp Cheddar Cheese

Directions:

1. Preheat your grill to 300 degrees. Set it up for indirect heat.

2. Divide your ground beef into equal amounts and make them into large balls.

3. Push a can into your ball and smush it.

4. Using your own hand, form the meat around your can, making sure to push it up evenly around your can.

5. Wrap 2 pieces of bacon around the base of your meat.

6. Extract your can and fill the hole with whatever you'd like.

7. In this example, we used green peppers, onions, brussels sprouts, and mushrooms.

8. Top it with your cheese.

9. Place on your grill and cook with indirect heat for approximately 1 hour.

10. Take off your grill.

11. Serve!

Juicy Sliders

Ingredients:

- Onion Powder
- Garlic
- Salt
- Pepper
- 1 Egg
- 8 ounces of Cheddar Cheese
- 1 pound of Ground Beef
- Dash of Worcestershire Sauce

Directions:

1. Mix your eggs, spices, and beef.
2. Divide your meat into patties of 1 1/2 ounces.
3. Add a 1/2 ounce of cheese to each of your patties.
4. Combine two of your patties to form one burger.
5. Use your hands to meld the two patties together.

6. Heat oil on high and then fry your burgers to your desired level.

7. Top with your cheese and your desired toppings.

8. Serve!

Bacon Wrapped Brats

Ingredients:

- 4 slices of Cheese
- 4 Brats
- 4 Romaine Lettuce Leafs
- 4 Bacon Slices
- 12-ounce Beers

Directions:

1. Place your brats in your pot. Cover it with your beer.
2. Boil for approximately 10 minutes.
3. Remove your brats and wrap them with your bacon.
4. Grill your bacon wrapped brats until your bacon gets crisp.
5. Serve!

Flank Steak Pinwheels

Ingredients:

- 8 ounces of Fresh Spinach
- Italian Seasoning
- 2 pounds of Flank Steak
- 16 ounces of Mozzarella Cheese

Directions:

1. Preheat your oven to 350 degrees.
1. 2.Place your flank steak so your grain is going right to left.
2. Square your flank and remove the hard fat deposits.
3. Using a sharp knife, butterfly your steak.
4. Be sure to cut parallel to your cutting board leaving about an inch not cut.
5. Always cut along the grain.
6. Open your steak, using your knife to finish off the cut so a 1/2 is still connected.

7. Lay your steak flat. Grain needs to be facing up and down your cutting board.

8. Season each side with Italian seasoning.

9. Spread your mozzarella cheese over your steak. Leave an inch on one of your sides for wrapping.

10. Lay down 2 layers of spinach.

11. Roll your steak. Be sure to keep it tight, rolling it with your grain.

12. Cut 6 pieces of twine and then tie off 6 sections spaced evenly.

13. Cut out your pinwheels carefully by cutting between twine pieces.

14. Place in your Pyrex baking dish over a layer of spinach.

15. Cook for approximately 25 minutes.

16. Broil for about 3 minutes until your cheese is bubbly.

17. Serve!

Fat Burning Ginger Steak

Ingredients:

- 1 clove of Crushed Garlic
- 1 tablespoon of Olive Oil
- 1 teaspoon of Ground Ginger
- 2 Sirloin Steaks (Each 4 Ounces)
- 4 tablespoons of Apple Cider Vinegar
- 1 Diced Small Onion
- 2 Small Diced Tomatoes
- Pepper
- Salt

Directions:

1. Place your oil in your large-sized skillet. Brown your steaks over a medium-high heat.
2. Once each side is seared, add in your tomatoes, garlic, and onion.
3. In your bowl, add your salt, pepper, and ginger into your vinegar and then add your

mixture to your skillet. Stir together well to combine.

4. Cover your skillet. Turn your heat to low and allow it to simmer until your liquids are completely evaporated.

5. Serve!

Stuffed & Seared Flank Steak

Ingredients:

- 1/2 teaspoon of Garlic Powder
- 1/2 teaspoon of Onion Powder
- 1/2 teaspoon of Pepper
- 1/2 teaspoon of Salt
- 2 Flank Steaks
- 16 ounces of Spinach
- 7 ounces of Roasted Red Peppers
- 1 Egg Yolk
- 4 ounces of Bleu Cheese
- 2 tablespoons of Almond Flour

Directions:

1. Place the grain of your flank steak vertically.
2. Butterfly your steak cutting from right to left.
3. Microwave your frozen spinach and then drain any liquid.
4. Slice your roasted red peppers.

93

5. Combine your remaining ingredients with your spinach. Mix together well.

6. Spread your mixture over your steak and then roll with your grain.

7. Truss your steak with some cotton twine.

8. Wrap it with saran wrap. Marinate it for approximately 30 minutes.

9. Cook for approximately 35 minutes at 425 degrees.

10. Broil steak for around 10 minutes. Rotate steak after approximately 5 minutes.

11. Cover it with your foil. Rest for approximately 10 minutes.

12. Serve!

Avocado Bacon Chicken Salad

Ingredients:

- 2 cup thinly sliced scallions
- 2 cup diced celery
- 1/4 cup caesar dressing
- table salt and ground black pepper, to taste
- 2 cups cooked chopped chicken
- 6 slices cooked bacon, crumbled
- 1 large avocado, chopped
- 2 cup shredded cheddar cheese

Directions:

1. Toss & Serve: Toss all ingredients together in large salad bowl until well-mixed.
2. Season with salt and pepper to taste and stir in extra dressing, if desired.
3. Serve promptly or store leftovers.

Keto Yogurt

Ingredients:

Dairy Free:

- 405 ml Coconut Cream
- 1 tsp Guar Gum
- 2 Whole Probiotic Pills Powdered Form

Whole Milk:

- 1 Liter Full Fat Milk
- 2 Whole Probiotic Pills Powdered Form

Directions:

Dairy Free:

1. Pour the coconut cream into a saucepan, add the guar gum and begin to slowly heat the milk until it begins to boil.
2. Once its boiling, keep it simmering at boil for 7 mins.
3. Remove from the stove and let it cool until it reaches 42 C (108 F).

4. Then transfer into a glass jar, stir in the probiotic tablet powder with a steralised spoon, then cover with a section of cheesecloth with a rubber band around the top.

5. Let it sit in a warm place for 48 hours. (You could also pour this into a thermos to keep the warmth at or around 42 C for longer).

6. You want the teperature to stay at or close to 42 C (108F).

Whole Milk Version:

1. Add 1 Litre of full fat milk to a saucepan and proceed the same as above.

2. Instead of letting it sit for 48 hours, only let it sit for 12 hours.

3. If you want it thicker, remove the clear whey protein from the mix by passing the room temperature liquid through a cheese cloth.

Paleo Baked Rosemary Salmon

Ingredients:

- 1/4 cup (4 tablespoons) olive oil
- 1 tsp salt (optional or to taste)
- 2 salmon fillets (fresh or defrosted)
- 1 tablespoon fresh rosemary leaves

Directions:

1. Preheat the oven to 350F (175C).
2. Mix the olive oil, rosemary, and salt together in a bowl.
3. Rub the mixture onto the salmon fillets.
4. Wrap each fillet in a piece of aluminium foil with some of the remaining mixture.
5. Bake for 25-30 minutes.

Low-Carb Zucchini Pizza Casserole

Ingredients:

- 1 1/2 tsp dried basil
- 1 1/2 tsp oregano
- 1/4 tsp salt
- 1 tsp ground sage
- 1 tsp ground thyme
- 1 tsp red pepper flakes
- 15 pepperonis
- 4 cups (~16 oz) shredded zucchini
- 2 cups shredded mozzarella cheese, divided
- 1 1/4 cup shredded cheddar cheese, divided
- 2/3 cup grated parmesan cheese
- 2 eggs
- 1 lb ground beef
- 7 oz Rao's Pizza Sauce

Materials:

- 9 x 13 casserole pan

- Food processor
- Nut milk bag or cheesecloth
- Electric mixer (optional)

Directions:

1. Preheat oven to 375 degrees and coat 9 x 13 casserole pan with nonstick cooking spray.

2. Pulse zucchini in a food processor until finely shredded.

3. Transfer zucchini to a nut milk bag or cheesecloth and squeeze to remove excess liquid. Set aside.

4. To a large mixing bowl, add shredded zucchini, 1 cup mozzarella, and 3/4 cup cheddar, parmesan, and eggs and mix with a spoon or electric mixer.

5. Transfer mixture to prepared casserole pan and press into even layer. Bake 20 minutes.

6. Meanwhile, brown ground beef in a pan over medium heat.

7. Drain excess grease, pour in tomato sauce, add spices, and stir until all ingredients are well-incorporated.

8. After the base layer is finished baking, pour beef and tomato mixture on top.

9. Sprinkle remaining mozzarella and cheddar on top and then add pepperonis.

10. Return casserole pan to oven and bake for 23-25 minutes.

11. Allow to cool fully before cutting and serving.

Boiled Eggs With Thai Dipping Sauce

Ingredients:

- 2 Tbsp fresh lime juice
- 2 tsp fish sauce
- 1 tsp Monkfruit / Erythritol Sweetener
- 5 large eggs
- 1/4 cup green onions sliced, (scallions)
- 1 medium red cayenne chilli sliced, (remove seeds for mild)

Directions:

1. Place a medium sized pot 1/3 filled with water onto the stove. Bring to the boil
2. Once water is boiling, gently place the eggs into the hot water, and cook for 5 minutes (8 minutes for hard boil)
3. While the eggs are cooking, slice the green onions and chili, set aside.
4. Into a small bowl, mix together the lime juice, fish sauce and erythritol

102

5. Remove the eggs from the hot water, run under cold water for 1 minute and peal shells.

6. Slice in half and place into a wide bowl.

7. Place the lime dipping sauce into the middle, and cover with green onions and chili.

8. Dip the eggs into the dipping sauce, and enjoy.

Keto Loaded Cauliflower Salad

Ingredients:

- 1/2 cup mayonnaise or, for egg-free, omit and use additional 1/4 cup sour cream
- 1 cup (4 oz) shredded extra sharp cheddar cheese
- 1/3 cup finely chopped green onions, divided
- 1 tbsp hot sauce
- 1/2 tsp paprika, divided
- 5 slices bacon
- 1 medium head cauliflower (~20 oz), chopped into small florets
- 2 tbsp avocado oil
- 1 tsp minced garlic
- 1/8 tsp black pepper
- 1/8 tsp salt
- 1 cup sour cream

Directions:

1. Preheat oven to 400 degrees and line baking sheet with foil.

2. In a large skillet over medium heat, cook bacon until crisp.

3. Transfer cooked bacon to a paper towel-lined plate to de-grease.

4. Once cool, crumble bacon. Set aside.

5. In a mixing bowl, stir together cauliflower florets, avocado oil, minced garlic, pepper, and salt.

6. Pour cauliflower onto prepared baking sheet and bake until lightly golden, about 15-20 minutes.

7. Remove from oven and allow cauliflower to cool completely.

8. In a mixing bowl, stir together cooled baked cauliflower, sour cream, and mayonnaise.

9. Fold in crumbled bacon, shredded cheddar, ¼ cup chopped green onions, hot sauce, and 1/8 tsp paprika.

10. Chill in refrigerator for at least 2 hours prior to serving.

11. Garnish with remaining chopped green onions and paprika. Serve chilled and enjoy!

Butter Coffee

Ingredients:

- 2 cups unsalted butter
- 1 tbsp of MCT oil or coconut oil
- 1 cup freshly made hot coffee

Directions:

1. In a mixer, combine both ingredients.
2. Blend until frothy and creamy.
3. Immediately serve.

Keto Roast Beef And Cheddar Plate

Ingredients:

- 1 tbsp mustard from Dijon
- 2 oz. Lettuce (11/2 cups)
- 2 tablespoons of extra virgin olive oil
- Salt and pepper
- 7 oz. Roast beef deli, wrapped
- 5 oz. Cheddar cheese (11/4 cups), sliced into finger-like slices
- Avocado, diced 1 (7 oz.)
- 6 sliced radishes
- 1 (1/2 oz.) scallion, cut off at an angle
- 1/2 cup of mayonnaise

Directions:

1. On a tray, put the roasted beef, cheese, avocado, scallion, and radishes.
2. Serve with salad, vinegar, olive oil, and a delicious dollop of mayonnaise.

Keto Fried Salmon With Broccoli And Cheese

Ingredients:

- 1 cup sliced cheddar cheese (4 oz.)
- 11⁄2 pounds of trout, boneless fillets
- 1 lime (optional)
- Broccoli 1 lb
- 3 oz. Butter
- Salt and pepper

Directions:

1. Preheat the oven, ideally using the broiler setting, 400 ° F (200 ° C).

2. Break the broccoli into smaller florets and let it boil for a few minutes in lightly salted water.

3. Making sure that the broccoli retains its chewy texture and delicate hue.

4. Drain the broccoli and discard the water that is boiling.
5. Put aside, exposed, to allow the steam to evaporate for a minute or two.
6. In a well-greased baking dish, put the drained broccoli in it.
7. To taste, incorporate butter and pepper.
8. Sprinkle on top of the broccoli with the cheese and bake for 15-20 minutes in the oven or until the cheese is golden.
9. Meanwhile, season the salmon with salt and pepper and fried in tonnes of butter on either side for a few minutes.
10. In the same pan, the lime may be fried or eaten raw.
11. On an outdoor barbecue, this step can also be accomplished.

Keto Coconut Porridge

Ingredients:

- 1 oz. Coconut oil or butter
- 4 tbsp cream of coconut
- 1 egg, pounded
- 1 tablespoon coconut flour
- 1⁄4 tsp of soil psyllium husk powder
- 1⁄4 tsp of salt

Directions:

1. Combine the egg, coconut flour, psyllium husk powder and salt in a shallow dish.
2. Melt the butter and coconut milk over low heat.
3. Whisk in the egg mixture gently, mixing until a smooth, dense texture is obtained.
4. Serve with milk or cream containing coconut.
5. Cover a few fresh or frozen berries with your porridge and enjoy it!

Keto Shrimp And Artichoke Plate

Ingredients:

- 1/2 cup of mayonnaise
- 2 cups of baby spinach (2 oz.)
- 4 tablespoons olive oil
- Salt and pepper
- Four eggs
- 11 oz. Shrimp fried and peeled
- 14 oz. Artichokes Canned
- 6 tomatoes sun-dried in oil

Directions:

1. You start by cooking the eggs. Whether you prefer them fluffy or hardboiled, lower them carefully into boiling water and simmer for 4-8 minutes.

2. When they're finished, cool the eggs for 1-2 minutes in ice-cold water; this will make it easier to extract the shell.

3. Place the eggs, seafood, artichokes, mayonnaise, spinach, and sun-dried tomatoes on a dish.

4. Drizzle over the spinach with olive oil—season with salt and pepper to taste and then serve.

Keto Chicken Casserole

Ingredients:

- 2 cup of milk for extreme whipping
- 1/2 cup of cream cheese
- 3 tbsp of green pesto
- 1 tablespoon lemon juice
- Salt and pepper
- 11/2 oz. Butter
- 2 lbs of skinless, boneless thighs of chicken, sliced into bite-size parts
- 6 oz. Leeks, sliced thinly
- 4 oz. Cherry tomatoes, sliced in half
- 2 lb of cauliflower, sliced into tiny florets
- 2 cups (8 oz.) of cheddar cheese, shredded

Directions:

1. Preheat the furnace to 200 °C (400 °F).
2. Pair the pesto and lemon juice with milk and cream cheese—salt to taste and pepper.

3. Melt the butter in a wide pan over medium to high heat.

4. Stir in the chicken, season with salt and pepper, and fry until the chicken turns golden brown.

5. "Put the chicken in an oiled baking sheet of 9 x 13" (23 x 33 cm) oiled baking dish and add the cream mixture into it.

6. Top with leek, onion, and cauliflower chicken.

7. Spread on top of the cheese and bake for at least 30 minutes in the middle of the oven or until the chicken is thoroughly cooked.

8. If the casserole is in danger of being burnt, until it is finished, cover it with a piece of foil of aluminum, decrease the heat and cook for a little longer.

Keto Egg Muffins

Ingredients:

- 2 tablespoons of red pesto or green pesto (optional)
- Salt and pepper
- 11/2 cups (6 oz.) cheddar cheese shredded
- 2 (1 oz.) scallions, finely chopped
- 5 oz. Bacon or salami fried, chopped
- Twelve eggs

Directions:

1. 175°C (350°F)Preheat the oven too.
2. Line a non-adhesive muffin pan, insertable baking cups, or grease a buttered silicone muffin tin (two muffins per serving).
3. To the bottom of the tin, apply scallions and chorizo.

4. Whisk the pesto, salt, and pepper along with the shells.

5. Attach and whisk in the cheese.

6. On top of the scallions and chorizo, mix in the batter.

7. Depending on the scale of the muffin pan, bake for 15–20 minutes.

Keto Cauliflower Soup With Crispy Pancetta

Ingredients:

- 4 cups chicken broth or stock of vegetables
- 7 oz. Cheese with cream cheese
- 1 tbsp mustard from Dijon
- 4 oz. Unsalted butter
- 2 tsp of salt
- 1/2 tsp of pepper
- Cauliflower of 1 lb, split into small florets, divided
- 1 tbsp of butter
- 7 oz. diced pancetta or bacon
- 3 oz. Pecans, chopped coarsely
- 1 teaspoon of paprika or smoked chili powder

Directions:

1. Cut a bunch of florets of cauliflower into 1/4 inch bits.

2. Put the butter in a medium-sized saute pan over medium-high heat (approximately 10" or 25 cm).

3. Attach bits of diced cauliflower and pancetta. Sauté until the pancetta becomes crispy or for around 8-10 minutes.

4. Stir in the pecans and paprika for the last few minutes. Only put aside.

5. Apply the broth to a medium-sized soup pot and the remaining cauliflower florets.

6. Protect and bring to a simmer for a few minutes, at elevated pressure.

7. Reduce the temperature and add the cream cheese, mustard, butter, salt, and pepper to a medium amount.

8. Combine the ingredients to the desired consistency using an immersion blender; mixing the mixture for a longer period will yield a creamier broth.

9. Spoon the soup into serving containers, then coat the mixture with the pancetta-pecan.

Keto Cheeseburger

Ingredients:

Salsa:

- 2 tomatoes (8 oz.)
- 2 scallions (1 oz.)
- 1 avocado (7 oz.)
- 1 tablespoon of olive oil
- 2 tbsp of fresh coriander, chopped
- Salt, for taste
- Hamburgers
- Ground beef 11/2 lbs •
- 12 cups (7 oz.) of shredded and split cheddar cheese
- 2 tsp powder of garlic
- 2 teaspoons of onion powder
- 2 tsp of powder paprika

- 2 tbsp of fresh oregano, finely chopped
- 2 oz. For frying, butter

The Toppings:

- 4 tbsp jalapeños pickled, diced
- 2 oz. Pickles from sliced dill
- 4 tbsp mustard from Dijon
- 5 oz. Lettuce (4 cups)
- 2 cup of mayonnaise
- 5 oz. Bacon fried, crumbled

Directions:

1. Chop up the salsa ingredients in a little bowl and stir them together. Only put aside.

2. Mix half the cheese into the ground beef and season with a hand or wooden spoon until mixed.

3. Create four burgers and, if you like, cook them in a pan or grill—season with salt and pepper and, in the end, but the remaining cheese on top.

4. Serve with mayo, sausage, pickled jalapeños, dill pickle and mustard on top of the lettuce.

5. And don't worry about the homemade sauce!

Boiled Eggs With Mayonnaise

Ingredients:

- 2 oz. Green asparagus ingredients (optional)
- 8 eggs
- 1/2 cup of mayonnaise

Directions:

1. In a kettle, put water to a boil.
2. Optional: Make tiny wholes with an egg piercer in the shells.
3. This helps avoid the cracking of eggs when cooking.
4. Place the eggs carefully in the water.
5. For soft-boiled eggs, cook the eggs for 5–6 minutes, 6–8 minutes for medium and 8–10 minutes for hardboiled eggs.
6. And mayonnaise, serve.

Keto Caesar Salad

Ingredients:

Dressing:

- 1/2 cup of mayonnaise
- 1 tbsp mustard from Dijon
- 1/2 lemon, zest and juice
- 1/4 cup grated shredded Parmesan cheese (2/3 oz.)
- 2 tbsp of finely chopped anchovy fillets
- 1 garlic clove, pressed or finely chopped
- Salt and pepper

The Salad:

- 3 oz. With pancakes
- 7 oz. Lettuce from Romaine, chopped
- 1/2 cup (11/3 oz.) of Parmesan shredded cheese
- 12 oz. Bone-in chicken breasts with skin
- Salt and pepper

- 1 tablespoon of olive oil

Directions:

1. 175°C (350°F) Preheat the oven.

2. Mix a whisk or an immersion blender with the ingredients for the dressing. Set in the refrigerator aside.

3. In a greased baking dish, put the chicken breasts.

4. Season the salt and pepper with the chicken and drizzle on top with olive oil or melted butter.

5. Bake in the oven for about 20 minutes or until the chicken is completely cooked.

6. If you like, you can prepare the chicken on the stovetop as well.

7. Till crisp, fried the bacon, place lettuce on two plates as a foundation.

8. Cover with the fried, crumbled bacon and the sliced chicken.

9. Finish off with a generous dollop of dressing and a strong parmesan cheese grating.

Parsnip Chips

Ingredients:

- 1 tablespoon parsley, chopped
- Salt and black pepper, to taste
- 1 garlic clove, minced
- 2 cups parsnips, sliced
- 3 tablespoons olive oil
- 1 cup natural yogurt
- 1 teaspoon lime juice

Directions:

1. Preheat the oven to 300ºF (150ºC). Set parsnip on a baking sheet; toss with garlic powder, 1 tablespoon of olive oil, and salt.
2. Bake for 15 minutes, tossing once halfway through, until slices are crisp and browned.
3. In a bowl, mix yogurt, lime juice, black pepper, 2 tablespoons of olive oil, garlic, and salt until well combined.
4. Serve the chips with yogurt dip.

Prosciutto Wrapped Basil Mozzarella

Ingredients:

- 18 basil leaves
- 18 Mozzarella ciliegine (about 8½ ounces / 241 g in total)
- 6 thin prosciutto slices

Directions:

1. Cut the prosciutto slices into three strips. Place basil leaves at the end of each strip.
2. Top with Mozzarella.
3. Wrap the Mozzarella in prosciutto.
4. Secure with toothpicks.

Liverwurst Truffles

Ingredients:

- 1/2 cup pistachios, chopped
- 1 teaspoon Dijon mustard
- 6 ounces (170 g) cream cheese
- 8 bacon slices, cooked and chopped
- 8 ounces (227 g) Liverwurst

Directions:

1. Combine liverwurst and pistachios in the bowl of your food processor.
2. Pulse until smooth.
3. Whisk the cream cheese and mustard in another bowl.
4. Make 12 balls out of the liverwurst mixture.
5. Make a thin cream cheese layer over.
6. Coat with bacon pieces.
7. Arrange on a plate and refrigerate for 30 minutes.

Chorizo And Asparagus Traybake

Ingredients:

- 4 ounces (113 g) Spanish chorizo, sliced
- Salt and black pepper to taste
- 1/2 cup chopped parsley
- 2 tablespoons olive oil
- A bunch of asparagus, ends trimmed and chopped

Directions:

1. Preheat your oven to 325ºF (163ºC) and grease a baking dish with olive oil.
2. Add in the asparagus and season with salt and black pepper.
3. Stir in the chorizo slices. Bake for 15 minutes until the chorizo is crispy.
4. Arrange on a serving platter and serve sprinkled with parsley.

Jalapeño And Zucchini Frittata Cups

Ingredients:

- 1 teaspoon dried oregano
- 2 tablespoons olive oil
- 2 green onions, chopped
- 1 garlic clove, minced
- 1 jalapeño pepper, chopped
- 1 carrot, chopped
- 1 zucchini, shredded
- 2 tablespoons Mozzarella cheese, shredded
- 8 eggs, whisked
- Salt and black pepper, to taste

Directions:

1. Sauté green onions and garlic in warm olive oil over medium heat for 3 minutes.
2. Stir in carrot, zucchini, and jalapeño pepper, and cook for 4 more minutes.

3. Remove the mixture to a lightly greased baking pan with a nonstick cooking spray.

4. Top with Mozzarella cheese.

5. Cover with the whisked eggs; season with oregano, black pepper, and salt.

6. Bake in the oven for about 20 minutes at 360ºF (182ºC).

Baked Romano Zucchini Rounds

Ingredients:

- Sea salt and ground black pepper, to taste

- 2 pounds (907 g) zucchini, sliced into rounds

- 1 cup Romano cheese, shredded

- 2 tablespoons olive oil

- 2 eggs

- 1 teaspoon smoked paprika

Directions:

1. Begin by preheating an oven to 420ºF (216ºC).

2. Coat a rimmed baking sheet with Silpat mat or parchment paper.

3. In a mixing bowl, whisk the olive oil with eggs.

4. Add in the paprika, salt, and black pepper.

5. Now, dip the zucchini slices into the egg mixture.

6. Top with the shredded Romano cheese.

7. Arrange the zucchini rounds on the baking sheet; bake for 15 minutes until they are golden.

8. Serve at room temperature.

Herbed Prawn And Veggie Skewers

Ingredients:

- 1 teaspoon fresh rosemary
- 2 tablespoons fresh lime juice
- 2 tablespoons cilantro, chopped
- 2 bell peppers, diced
- 1 cup cherry tomatoes
- 2 tablespoons olive oil
- 1 pound (454 g) king prawns, deveined and cleaned
- Sea salt and ground black pepper, to taste
- 1 teaspoon garlic powder
- 1 tablespoon fresh sage, minced

Directions:

1. Heat the olive oil in a wok over a moderately high heat.
2. Now, cook the prawns for 7 to 8 minutes, until they have turned pink.

3. Stir in the seasonings and cook an additional minute, stirring frequently.
4. Remove from the heat and toss with the lime juice and fresh cilantro.
5. Tread the prawns onto bamboo skewers, alternating them with peppers and cherry tomatoes.
6. Serve on a serving platter. Bon appétit!

Deviled Eggs With Roasted Peppers

Ingredients:

- 1 teaspoon stone-ground mustard
- 1 garlic clove, minced
- Sea salt, to taste
- 1 teaspoon red pepper flakes
- 10 eggs
- 1/2 cup sour cream
- 1/2 cup roasted red pepper, chopped
- 2 tablespoons olive oil

Directions:

1. Arrange the eggs in a saucepan.
2. Pour in water (1-inch above the eggs) and bring to a boil.
3. Heat off and let it sit, covered, for 9 to 10 minutes.
4. When the eggs are cool enough to handle, peel away the shells; rinse the eggs under running water.

5. Separate egg whites and yolks.

6. Mix the egg yolks with the sour cream,
   roasted pepper, olive oil, mustard, garlic, and
   salt.

7. Stuff the eggs, arrange on a nice serving
   platter, and garnish with red pepper flakes.
   Enjoy!

Greek-Style Ricotta Olive Dip

Ingredients:

- 1 teaspoon shallot powder
- 1 teaspoon garlic salt
- 1 teaspoon black pepper
- 4 tablespoons cilantro, minced
- 10 ounces (284 g) ricotta cheese
- 4 tablespoons Greek yogurt
- 1 teaspoon cayenne pepper
- 4 tablespoons olives, sliced

Directions:

1. Thoroughly combine the ricotta cheese, Greek yogurt, cayenne pepper, olives, shallot powder, garlic salt, and black pepper in a mixing bowl.
2. Transfer to a nice serving bowl.
3. Garnish with cilantro, serve and enjoy your party!

Lettuce Wraps With Ham And Tomato

Ingredients:

- 10 thin ham slices
- 1 tomato, chopped
- 1 red chili pepper, chopped
- 10 Boston lettuce leaves, washed and rinsed well
- 1 tablespoon lemon juice, freshly squeezed
- 10 tablespoons cream cheese

Directions:

1. Drizzle lemon juice over the lettuce leaves.
2. Spread cream cheese over the lettuce leaves.
3. Add a ham slice on each leaf.
4. Divide chopped tomatoes between the lettuce leaves.
5. Top with chili peppers and arrange on a nice serving platter. Bon appétit!

Blue Cheese And Ranch Dip

Ingredients:

- 1 tablespoon lime juice
- Freshly ground black pepper, to taste
- 2 tablespoons ranch seasoning
- 1 cup Greek-style yogurt
- 1 cup blue cheese, crumbled
- 1 cup mayonnaise

Directions:

1. In a mixing bowl, thoroughly combine all ingredients until well incorporated.
2. Serve well chilled with your favorite keto dippers. Bon appétit!

Chicken Wings With Ranch Dressing

Ingredients:

- 1 cup mayonnaise
- 1 teaspoon lemon juice
- 1 tablespoon fresh parsley, minced
- 1 clove garlic, minced
- 2 tablespoons onion, finely chopped
- 1/2 teaspoon dry mustard
- Sea salt and ground black pepper, to taste
- 2 pounds (907 g) chicken wings, pat dry
- Nonstick cooking spray
- Sea salt and cayenne pepper, to taste
- 1/2 cup sour cream
- 1/2 cup coconut milk

Directions:

1. Start by preheating your oven to 420ºF (216ºC).
2. Spritz the chicken wings with a cooking spray.

3. Sprinkle the chicken wings with salt and cayenne pepper.

4. Arrange the chicken wings on a parchment-lined baking pan.

5. Bake in the preheated oven for 50 minutes or until the wings are golden and crispy.

6. In the meantime, make the dressing by mixing all of the above ingredients.

7. Serve with warm wings.

Mozzarella Meatballs

Ingredients:

- 2 tablespoons shallots, chopped
- 4 ounces (113 g) Mozzarella string cheese, cubed
- 1 ripe tomato, puréed
- Salt and ground black pepper, to taste
- 1 pound (227 g) ground pork
- 1 pound (454 g) ground turkey
- 1 garlic clove, minced
- 4 tablespoons pork rinds, crushed

Directions:

1. In a mixing bowl, thoroughly combine all ingredients, except for the cheese.
2. Shape the mixture into bite-sized balls.
3. Press 1 cheese cube into the center of each ball.
4. Place the meatballs on a parchment-lined baking sheet.

5. Bake in the preheated oven at 350ºF (180ºC) for 18 to 25 minutes. Bon appétit!

Italian Cheddar Cheese Crisps

Ingredients:

- 1 teaspoon cayenne pepper
- 1 teaspoon Italian seasoning
- 1 cup sharp Cheddar cheese, grated
- 1/2 teaspoon ground black pepper

Directions:

1. Start by preheating an oven to 400ºF (205ºC).
2. Line a baking sheet with a parchment paper.
3. Mix all of the above ingredients until well combined.
4. Then, place tablespoon-sized heaps of the mixture onto the prepared baking sheet.
5. Bake at the preheated oven for 8 minutes, until the edges start to brown.
6. Allow the cheese crisps to cool slightly; then, place them on paper towels to drain the excess fat. Enjoy!

Deviled Eggs With Chives

Ingredients:

- 1 tablespoon tomato purée, no sugar added
- 1 teaspoon balsamic vinegar
- Sea salt and freshly ground black pepper, to taste
- ¼ teaspoon cayenne pepper
- 2 tablespoons chives, chopped
- 8 eggs
- 2 tablespoons cream cheese
- 1 teaspoon Dijon mustard
- 1 tablespoon mayonnaise

Directions:

1. Place the eggs in a single layer in a saucepan.
2. Add water to cover the eggs and bring to a boil.
3. Cover, turn off the heat, and let the eggs stand for 15 minutes.

4. Drain the eggs and peel them under cold running water.
5. Slice the eggs in half lengthwise; remove the yolks and thoroughly combine them with cream cheese, mustard, mayo, tomato purée, vinegar, salt, black, and cayenne pepper.
6. Next, divide the yolk mixture among egg whites.
7. Garnish with fresh chives and enjoy!

Hearty Burger Dip

Ingredients:

- 1 cup Provolone cheese, grated
- 2 ounces (57 g) tomato purée
- 1 teaspoon mustard
- 1 teaspoon dried oregano
- 1 teaspoon dried basil
- 1/2 teaspoon dried marjoram
- 1/2 pound (113 g) ground pork
- 1/2 pound (113 g) ground turkey
- 1 red onion, chopped
- 1 garlic clove, minced
- 1 serrano pepper, chopped
- 1 bell pepper, chopped
- 2 ounces (57 g) sour cream

Directions:

1. Place all of the above ingredients, except for the sour cream and Provolone cheese in your slow cooker.
2. Cook for 1 hour 30 minutes at Low setting.
3. Afterwards, fold in sour cream and cheese.
4. Serve warm with celery sticks if desired.
5. Bon appétit!

Lemony Bacon Chips

Ingredients:

- 1 teaspoon Ranch seasoning mix
- 1 tablespoon hot sauce
- 2 pounds (680 g) bacon, cut into 1-inch squares
- 1/2 cup lemon juice

Directions:

1. Toss the bacon squares with the lemon juice, Ranch seasoning mix, and hot sauce.
2. Arrange the bacon squares on a parchment-lined baking sheet.
3. Roast in the preheated oven at 375ºF (190ºC) approximately 10 minutes or until crisp.
4. Let it cool completely before storing. Bon appétit!

Parmesan Crab Dip

Ingredients:

- 1 tablespoon chopped fresh parsley
- 2 teaspoons fresh lemon juice
- 2 teaspoons Sriracha sauce
- 1 teaspoon garlic powder
- 8 ounces (227 g) fresh lump crab meat
- Salt and pepper, to taste
- 4 ounces (113 g) cream cheese, softened
- 1 cup shredded Parmesan cheese, plus ½ cup extra for topping (optional)
- 1 cup mayonnaise
- 1/2 cup sour cream

Directions:

1. Preheat the oven to 375ºF (190ºC).
2. Combine all the ingredients except for the crabmeat in a mixing bowl and use a hand mixer to blend until smooth.

3. Put the crabmeat in a separate bowl, check for shells, and rinse with cold water, if needed.

4. Pat dry or allow to rest in a strainer until most of the water has drained.

5. Add the crabmeat to the bowl with the cream cheese mixture and gently fold to combine.

6. Taste for seasoning and add salt and pepper to taste, if needed.

7. Pour into an 8-inch round or square baking dish and bake for 25

8. minutes, until the cheese has melted and the dip is warm throughout.

9. If desired, top the dip with another ½ cup of Parmesan cheese and broil for 2 to 3 minutes, until the cheese has melted and browned slightly.

Ranch Chicken-Bacon Dip

Ingredients:

- 1 cup Buffalo sauce
- 1 cup ranch dressing
- Chopped green onions, for garnish (optional)
- 3 slices bacon
- 2 cups shredded cooked chicken
- 1 (8-ounce / 227-g) package cream cheese, softened

Directions:

1. Preheat the oven to 375ºF (190ºC).
2. In a skillet over medium heat, fry the bacon until crispy.
3. Set aside on a paper towel-lined plate to cool, then chop.
4. In a large bowl, combine the shredded chicken, cream cheese, Buffalo sauce, ranch dressing, and bacon; mix well. (If desired,

reserve some of the bacon to sprinkle on top, as pictured.)

5. Transfer the chicken mixture to a shallow 1-quart baking dish and bake for 20 minutes, until warm throughout.

6. Garnish with chopped green onions, if desired.

Classic Caprese Skewers

Ingredients:

- 9 grape tomatoes, halved

- 18 fresh basil leaves

- 8 ounces (227 g) ciliegini Mozzarella balls, drained and halved

Marinade:

- 1 tablespoon dried ground oregano

- 1 tablespoon fresh lemon juice

- Kosher salt and ground black pepper, to taste

- 1/2 cup extra-virgin olive oil

- 1 clove garlic, pressed or minced

- 1 tablespoon chopped fresh parsley

Directions:

1. In a medium-sized bowl, combine the Mozzarella balls with the marinade ingredients. Stir well and cover; place in the refrigerator to marinate for 1 hour.

2. To assemble, place a Mozzarella ball, a basil leaf (folded in half lengthwise if needed), and a grape tomato half on a toothpick.
3. Serve right away or store in the refrigerator until ready to serve.

Coconut Porridge With Strawberries

Ingredients:

- 1 pinch ground chia seeds
- 5 tbsp coconut cream
- 1 pinch salt
- Strawberries to serve
- Flax egg: 1 tbsp flax seed powder + 3 tbsp water
- 1 oz olive oil
- 1 tbsp coconut flour

Directions:

1. and Total Time: approx. 12 minutes
2. For flax egg, in a bowl, mix flax seed powder with water, and let soak for 5 minutes.
3. Place a saucepan over low heat and pour in olive oil, flax egg, flour, chia, coconut cream, and salt.
4. Cook, while stirring continuously until the desired consistency is achieved.

5. Top with strawberries.

Mexican Tofu Scramble

Ingredients:

- 1 tomato, finely chopped
- 2 tbsp chopped scallions
- Salt and black pepper to taste
- 1 tsp Mexican chili powder
- 3 oz grated Parmesan cheese
- 8 oz tofu, scrambled
- 2 tbsp butter
- 1 green bell pepper, chopped

Directions:

1. and Total Time: approx. 45 minutes
2. Melt butter in a skillet over medium heat.
3. Fry the tofu until golden brown, stirring occasionally, about 5 minutes.
4. Stir in bell pepper, tomato, scallions, and cook until the vegetables are soft, 4 minutes.
5. Season with salt, pepper, chili powder and stir in Parmesan cheese, about 2 minutes. Spoon

the scramble into a serving platter and serve warm.

No-Bread Avocado Sandwiches

Ingredients:

- 1 oz butter, softened
- 4 tofu slices
- 1 tsp chopped parsley
- 1 avocado, sliced
- 1 large red tomato, sliced
- 4 little gem lettuce leaves

Directions:

1. and Total Time: approx. 10 minutes
2. Arrange the lettuce on a flat serving plate.
3. Smear each leave with butter and arrange tofu slices on the leaves.
4. Top with the avocado and tomato slices.
5. Garnish the sandwiches with parsley and serve.

Blueberry Chia Pudding

Ingredients:

- 1 tbsp chopped walnuts
- 2 cup coconut milk
- 1 tsp vanilla extract
- 1 cup blueberries
- 2 tbsp chia seeds

Directions:

1. and Total Time: approx. 10 min + chilling time
2. In a blender, pour coconut milk, vanilla extract, and half of the blueberries.
3. Process the ingredients in high speed until the blueberries have incorporated into the liquid.
4. Mix in chia seeds.
5. Share the mixture into 2 breakfast jars, cover, and refrigerate for 4 hours to allow it to gel.
6. Garnish with the remaining blueberries and walnuts. Serve.

Creamy Sesame Bread

Ingredients:

- 2 tbsp psyllium husk powder
- 1 tsp salt
- 1 tsp baking powder1 tbsp sesame seeds
- 4 tbsp flax seed powder
- 1 cup cream cheese 5 tbsp sesame oil
- 1 cup coconut flour

Directions:

1. and Total Time: approx. 40 minutes
2. In a bowl, mix flax seed powder with 2 cups water until smoothly combined and set aside to soak for 5 minutes.
3. Preheat oven to 400 F. When the flax egg is ready, beat in cream cheese and 4 tbsp sesame oil until mixed.
4. Whisk in coconut flour, psyllium husk powder, salt, and baking powder until adequately blended.

5. Spread the dough in a greased baking tray.

6. Allow to stand for 5 minutes and then brush with remaining sesame oil.

7. Sprinkle with sesame seeds and bake the dough for 30 minutes.

8. Slice and serve.

Bulletproof Coffee

Ingredients:

- 1 tbsp coconut oil
- 2 tbsp unsalted butter
- 3 heaping tbsp ground bulletproof coffee beans

Directions:

1. and Total Time: approx. 3 minutes
2. Using a coffee maker, brew one cup of coffee with the ground coffee beans and 1 cup of water.
3. Transfer the coffee to a blender and add the coconut oil and butter.
4. Blend the mixture until frothy and smooth.

Breakfast Naan Bread

Ingredients:

- 1/2 cup olive oil
- 2 cups boiling water
- 8 oz butter
- 2 garlic cloves, minced
- 2 cup almond flour
- 2 tbsp psyllium husk powder
- 1 tsp salt
- 1 tsp baking powder

Directions:

1. and Total Time: approx. 25 minutes
2. In a bowl, mix almond flour, psyllium husk powder, ½ teaspoon of salt, and baking powder.
3. Mix in olive oil and boiling water to combine the ingredients like a thick porridge.
4. Stir and allow the dough rise for 5 minutes.

5. Divide the dough into 6 pieces and mold into balls.

6. Place the balls on a parchment paper and flatten.

7. Melt half of the butter in a frying pan over medium heat and fry the naan on both sides to have a golden color.

8. Transfer to a plate and keep warm. Add the remaining butter to the pan and sauté garlic until fragrant, about 1 minute.

9. Pour the garlic butter into a bowl and serve as a dip along with the naan.

Seeds Breakfast Loaf

Ingredients:

- 2 cup heavy cream 4 tbsp sesame oil
- 2 cup coconut flour
- 1 cup almond flour
- 3 tbsp baking powder
- 2 tbsp psyllium husk powder
- 1 tsp ground caraway seeds
- 1 tbsp poppy seeds
- 1 tsp salt
- 1 tsp mixed spices
- 6 eggs
- 1 cup cream cheese, softened
- 2 tbsp desiccated coconut
- 5 tbsp sesame seeds
- 1/2cup flaxseed
- 1/2 cup hemp seeds

Directions:

1. and Total Time: approx. 55 minutes
2. Preheat oven to 350 F. In a bowl, mix coconut and almond flours, baking powder, psyllium husk, desiccated coconut, sesame seeds, flaxseed, hemp seeds, ground caraway and poppy seeds, salt, and mixed spice.
3. In another bowl, whisk eggs, cream cheese, heavy cream, and sesame oil.
4. Pour the mixture into the dry ingredients and combine both into a smooth dough.
5. Pour the dough in a greased loaf pan.
6. Bake for 45 minutes.
7. Remove onto a rack and let cool.

Blackberry Chia Pudding

Ingredients:

- 7 tbsp chia seeds
- 1 cup fresh blackberries
- 3 tbsp chopped almonds Mint leaves to garnish
- 2 cups coconut milk
- 1 cup Greek yogurt
- 4 tsp sugar-free maple syrup
- 1 tsp vanilla extract

Directions:

1. and Total Time: approx. 45 minutes
2. In a bowl, combine coconut milk, Greek yogurt, sugar-free maple syrup, and vanilla extract until evenly combined.
3. Mix in the chia seeds. Puree half of blackberries in a bowl using a fork and stir in the yogurt mixture.

4. Share the mixture into medium mason jars, cover the lids and refrigerate for 30 minutes to thicken the pudding.

5. Remove the jars, take off the lid, and stir the mixture.

6. Garnish with remaining blackberries, almonds, and some mint leaves.

Blueberry Soufflé

Ingredients:

- 3 egg whites
- 1 tsp olive oil
- 1 lemon, zested
- 1 cup frozen blueberries
- 5 tbsp erythritol
- 4 egg yolks

Directions:

1. and Total Time: approx. 35 minutes
2. Pour blueberries, 2 tbsp erythritol and 1 tbsp water in a saucepan.
3. Cook until the berries soften and become syrupy, 8-10 minutes.
4. Set aside. Preheat oven to 350 F.
5. In a bowl, beat egg yolks and 1 tbsp of erythritol until thick and pale.
6. In another bowl, whisk egg whites until foamy.

7. Add in remaining erythritol and whisk until soft peak forms, 3-4 minutes.
8. Fold egg white mixture into egg yolk mix.
9. Heat olive oil in a pan over low heat.
10. Add in olive oil and pour in the egg mixture; swirl to spread.
11. Cook for 3 minutes and transfer to the oven; bake for 2-3 minutes or until puffed and set.
12. Plate soufflé and spoon blueberry sauce all over. Garnish with lemon zest.

Cheddar Biscuits

Ingredients:

- 2 eggs beaten
- 3 tbsp melted butter
- 2 cup grated cheddar cheese
- 3 cups almond flour
- 2 tsp baking powder

Directions:

1. and Total Time: approx. 30 minutes
2. Preheat oven to 350 F. Line a baking sheet with parchment paper.
3. In a bowl, mix flour, baking powder, and eggs until smooth.
4. Whisk in the melted butter and cheddar cheese until well combined.
5. Mold 12 balls out of the mixture and arrange on the sheet at 2-inch intervals.
6. Bake for 25 minutes until golden brown.
7. Remove, let cool, and serve.

Vanilla Buttermilk Pancakes

Ingredients:

- 1 vanilla pod
- 2 tbsp unsalted butter
- 2 tbsp olive oil
- 3 tbsp sugar-free maple syrup
- Greek yogurt to serve Blueberries to serve
- 1 cup almond flour
- 1 tsp baking powder
- 1 tbsp swerve sugar
- 1 cup buttermilk
- 1 lemon, juiced
- 3 eggs

Directions:

1. and Total Time: approx. 25 minutes
2. Into a bowl, mix almond flour, baking powder, and swerve sugar.
3. In a small bowl, whisk buttermilk, lemon juice, and eggs.

4. Combine the mixture with the flour mix until smooth.

5. Cut the vanilla pod open and scrape the beans into the flour mixture.

6. Stir to incorporate evenly.

7. In a skillet, melt a quarter each of the butter and olive oil and spoon in 1 ½ tablespoons of the pancake mixture into the pan.

8. Cook for 4 minutes or until small bubbles appear.

9. Flip and cook for 2 minutes or until set and golden.

10. Repeat cooking until the batter finishes using the remaining butter and olive oil in the same proportions.

11. Plate the pancakes, drizzle with maple syrup, top with a generous dollop of yogurt, and scatter some blueberries on top.

Berry & Mascarpone Bowl

Ingredients:

- 1 tsp liquid stevia
- 2 cups mascarpone cheese 1 cup raw pistachios
- 2 cups blueberries and raspberries
- 4 cups Greek yogurt

Directions:

1. and Total Time: approx. 10 minutes
2. Mix the yogurt, stevia, and mascarpone in a bowl until evenly combined.
3. Divide the mixture into 4 bowls, sprinkle the berries and pistachios on top and serve.

Avocado Halloumi Scones

Ingredients:

- 1 cup butter, cold
- 1 avocado, pitted and mashed
- 1 large egg
- 1/3 cup buttermilk
- 1 cup halloumi cheese, grated
- 2 cups almond flour
- 3 tsp baking powder

Directions:

1. and Total Time: approx. 35 minutes
2. Preheat oven to 350 F. Line a baking sheet with parchment paper.
3. In a bowl, combine flour and baking powder.
4. Add in butter and mix. Stir in halloumi cheese, and avocado.
5. Whisk the egg with buttermilk and stir in the halloumi mix.
6. Mold 8-10 scones out to the batter.

7. Place on the baking sheet and bake for 25 minutes or until the scones turn a golden color.

8. Let cool before serving.

Almond-Berry Pancakes With Sweet Syrup

Ingredients:

- 1 tbsp swerve sugar
- A pinch of cinnamon powder
- 1 egg
- 1 cup almond milk
- 2 tsp butter
- 1 cup Greek yogurt
- 1 handful of strawberries and raspberries, mashed
- 1 handful fresh strawberries and raspberries for topping
- 1 cup almond flour
- 1 tsp baking soda
- A pinch of salt

Directions:

1. and Total Time: approx. 25 minutes

2. In a bowl, combine almond flour, baking soda, salt, swerve sugar, and cinnamon.

3. Whisk in mashed berries, egg, and milk until smooth.

4. Melt ½ tsp of butter in a skillet and pour in 1 tbsp of the mixture into the pan.

5. Cook until small bubbles appear, flip, and cook until golden.

6. Transfer to a plate and proceed using up the remaining batter for pancakes.

7. Top pancakes with yogurt and whole berries.

Toast Sticks & Berry Yogurt Bowls

Ingredients:

- 2 eggs
- 1/2 tsp cinnamon powder
- 1/2 tsp nutmeg powder
- 2 tbsp almond milk
- 4 slices zero carb bread
- 2 tbsp butter 1 tbsp olive oil
- 2 cups Greek yogurt
- 2 tbsp sugar-free maple syrup
- 1 cup strawberries, halved
- 1 cup blueberries
- 1 cup raspberries

Directions:

1. and Total Time: approx. 15 min + chilling time
2. In a bowl, mix yogurt, maple syrup, and berries.
3. Chill for about 1 hour.

4. In another bowl, whisk eggs, cinnamon, nutmeg, and almond milk.

5. Set aside. Cut each bread slice into four strips.

6. Heat butter and olive oil in a skillet over medium heat.

7. Dip each strip into the egg mixture and fry in the skillet, flipping once until golden brown on both sides.

8. Transfer to a serving plate and serve warm.

CPSIA information can be obtained
at www.ICGtesting.com
Printed in the USA
LVHW041642220422
716950LV00024B/1567

9 781990 053405